THE LITTLE BOOK OF

BLISS

HOW TO
REACH
CLOUD
NINE

Patrick Whiteside

**Andrews McMeel
Publishing**

Kansas City

ISBN: 0-7407-2236-0

LIBRARY OF CONGRESS CATALOG NUMBER:

2001094776

First publication by Ebury Press in Great Britain 2000

For my patients,

For their patience,

With gratitude, affection,
and respect.

PREFACE

Many of the thousands of people who enjoyed *The Little Book of Happiness* discovered that it is better read from front to back as normal, rather than being dipped into at random. So it is with *The Little Book of Bliss*. A series of themes are introduced and developed page by page.

To those who are enlightened on the subject, life is like a kind of dance.

What happens when people fall or get tangled up when dancing? They stop briefly, collect themselves, regain their balance, and continue . . .

They dance on! When you go beyond a problem in this way, it is no longer a problem. If you go beyond all your problems, then you encounter bliss.

That moment in which someone regains equilibrium and poise, a sense of place and direction, is vital. Paradoxically then, in order to keep moving, we all have first to learn to be still. Keeping that inner stillness while in motion is the real secret of progress, of both success and enjoyment. This is true when dancing, and of course also in life. Awareness of others, especially those close to you, is important too. Keep moving, stay alert, and pay attention to those nearby and you will surely find bliss.

This is the basis of what I have written here in this book.

Patrick Whiteside

Go beyond . . .

Go beyond.

Go beyond!

Go beyond what?

Go beyond everything . . .

Go beyond!

To find happiness, bliss,

Go beyond everything . . .

Beyond even yourself!

Beyond your thoughts.

Beyond words . . .

Beyond even ideas.

Still the mind.

Be still . . .

Let it be!

Go beyond the senses.

Watch your mind . . .

Set it free!

How many minds
does someone have?

At any moment we have

Both many . . .

And one.

How many minds do we have?

Child mind, young mind,

Adult mind, old mind . . .

Glad mind, sad mind,

Dull mind, clear mind.

How many minds do we have?

Logical, rational . . . playful, creative,

Anxious, angry . . . calm, serene,

Grasping, selfish . . . Giving and kind.

Go beyond these distinctions . . .

Let all minds merge
into one!

Find contentment . . . Be happy . . .
Be still.

Go beyond every division, every
boundary . . .

In your thoughts.

Be mindful.

Bring your many minds
into one.

Beyond divisions, beyond
boundaries . . .

This is the meaning of wholeness.

This is the meaning of "integrity."

This is the road to happiness.

Be trustworthy, reliable . . .

Be at one!

Be still . . . Be at one . . .

Go beyond.

Travel on . . .

Travel on into bliss.

Do not worry if you do not yet understand.

Be still and let your mind do its work.

Ponder . . . persevere . . .

It will come.

You can be confident.

Be happy!

Seek wholeness, integrity!

Find one mind in yourself . . .

One mind with others . . .

One mind with the universe.

Seek integrity, wholeness!

Find one mind in yourself . . .

Find yourself . . .

In the single mind of eternity.

Seek yourself . . .

In the one mind of the cosmos,

And find the one mind
of the cosmos . . .

Within yourself.

Be happy . . .

Be at peace.

Be at peace!

Desire splits the mind . . .

Aversion splits the mind . . .

Likes and dislikes split and splinter
the mind.

Make it whole again!

Anger splinters the mind.

Bewilderment, doubt, guilt,
and shame . . .

These splinter the mind.

Go beyond feelings like these . . .

Heal your mind.

Make it whole.

Anger, desire, bewilderment,

Doubt, guilt, and shame

Split and splinter the mind . . .

But sorrow may restore happiness.

Sorrow sometimes brings healing.

Have you heard . . .

*"A day without tears
and without laughter . . .
Is a day wasted"?*

Sorrow, crying, tears . . . resolution!

The mind starts healing itself.

Sorrow, crying, tears . . .

And in time . . . Laughter!

With laughter, ease . . .

Anxiety fading away.

Let yourself go.

Give yourself to tears.

Little by little . . .

Feel the healing begin.

Then, go beyond your tears.

Do not try to hold on . . .

To what has already been lost.

Go beyond tears toward laughter,
release, relief . . .

Toward relief and the gaining
of wisdom.

When you survive a loss,

You will have learned
something new.

When you survive a loss,

You will have learned
something new . . .

About yourself,

About others,

About the world,

About life!

Laugh and cry every day,
and then . . .

If only for an instant . . .

Go beyond laughter and tears . . .

Go beyond, and enter the calm.

Enter the calm . . .

Reach wisdom's source.

Here is eternity . . . the moment
of your birth.

Enter the calm . . .

Reach wisdom's source!

Here is eternity . . . the moment too
of your death.

Go beyond distinction
between life and death!

If you find this hard to understand,

Do not worry and make it
a problem . . .

Leave it be . . .

Take a rest.

Life and death, both are holy . . .

Both are hallowed,

Both are sacred.

Even without dying may we not . . .

Enter the calm,

Enter the mystery,

Enter the joy?

Even without dying . . .

May we not enter the mystery . . .

Beyond pleasure and pain?

Even without dying
(the wise ones of old said) . . .

We may be reborn beyond life,

Beyond death . . .

And find our natural home.

Dwell in the present

And be reborn in happiness . . .

In bliss.

Even in the present you are
moving on . . . Going beyond!

We all go beyond every moment.

To be reborn every moment . . .

"In newness of life."

This is the way . . .

The way beyond sorrow . . .

Laugh! . . . Cry! . . . Live! . . . Die!

Beyond mirth and tears,

Beyond life and death . . .

Lies bliss, serenity, peace.

If you would like, pause . . .

Ponder on this.

Take a rest.

Who can avoid pain, physical
and emotional?

Who can avoid suffering?

No one!

Harsh but true . . .

Take stock, then go beyond this.

No one can avoid suffering.

What shall we do then

From the moment of birth . . .

Until our natural death?

What shall we do . . .

Moment by moment,

Hour by hour,

Day by day,

Month by month,

Year by year?

What shall we do to find
contentment, happiness?

How are we profitably to fill
the time?

What shall we do . . .

And . . . what shall we not do?

Live . . .

Live each moment.

This is what to do.

Live each moment
one at a time . . .

Hour by hour,

Day by day,

Week by week . . .

As best you can.

This is the way!

Live each moment one
at a time . . .

Live in hope.

Are there not plenty of choices?

It is good to recognize choices.

Each heart must beat,

And each must breathe . . . lifelong.

We have little choice about that.

Every day . . .

Let your body do its work.

Help it along.

Nourish it!

Let your body do its work.

Honor it as if it belonged to your beloved!

Cherish it . . .

As if it belonged to your child!

Let your body do its work.

Every day you must . . .

Clean it, groom it,

Feed it, void it,

Clothe it.

Do you have choices about these . . .

Cleaning, grooming, feeding,
voiding, clothing?

Make your choice and move on.

Choose, if you can, to be happy.

Let your body do its work . . .

Rest it and exercise it,

Exercise and rest it.

Strike a balance.

Exercise . . . work and play.

Rest . . . relax and sleep.

When the body is sleeping,

The mind is awake . . .

Preparing for happiness.

Pay attention to it on waking.

Dreams can be a precious gift.

Pay attention . . .

Why be in a hurry,

Each morning,

To arise?

When you are asleep

There is drowsiness, light sleep,
deep sleep . . .

And dreaming.

In deep sleep . . .

The body is refreshed.

In dreaming . . .

The mind is refreshed.

Let your mind go through
the cycles . . .

Drowsiness, light sleep,

Deep sleep and dreaming . . .

Four or five times a night.

If sleep is disturbed,

Are strong and painful emotions
at work?

Is there desire or hatred . . .

Anger, anxiety, confusion,
or doubt?

Is there shame, guilt,
or sorrow?

If sleep is disturbed,

Will your mind not also
be troubled . . .

When you are awake?

Distractions only work
for a while . . .

Until new miseries arise,

Or bad feelings grow worse.

Take your mind off your worries
and, sadly,

They will most likely return.

For happiness' sake,

Pay attention to disturbing and
painful emotions.

Be still and watch them settle.

Be still and watch them pass.

If you want to be happy . . .

Be still!

Be still . . . Practice.

Sit quietly for a while . . .

Undistracted . . .

Every day.

The passing of painful,
disturbing emotions

Leads to peace,

Leads to happiness . . .

Leads to happiness and peace . . .

Leads to bliss!

Now, what choices do you have
about work?

What do you like?

What are you good at?

What can you do that is useful?

The easiest choices are simple.

Explore your options.

Discover your abilities and work
to develop them . . .

Then your choices are simpler.

Explore your options.

Discover your limitations
and respect them . . .

If they cannot be overcome,

Then again, being fewer,
the choices are simpler.

This is the way!

Live each moment one at a time,

Guided by sacred knowledge . . .

By wisdom . . .

By the wisdom all are heirs to
at birth.

Be happy . . . Choose wisely!

Wisdom is sacred knowledge . . .

Inherited from the universe,

Accessible to all . . .

The basis of all knowledge.

Wisdom, sacred knowledge . . .

Is the basis of all knowledge.

From start to finish,

It is also the basis of science.

Wisdom is forceful . . .

Immediate and incontrovertible.

Also gentle, eternal . . .

A mystery!

Wisdom is immediate and personal,

Yet we share it . . .

It claims us all.

Somehow forceful, immediate,
personal,

Yet gentle, eternal, and universal . . .

Incontrovertible and mysterious
both . . .

How can this possibly be?

How can this mystery be?

Do not trouble yourself.

Go beyond the question . . .

The answer is . . . perfect wisdom.

What does this mean?

How can this be?

Do not even ask!

Do not trouble yourself with these
difficult questions . . .

Respect paradox . . . Revere mystery.

Absorb wisdom . . . Enter bliss!

Wisdom is beyond consensus.

It simply reflects the way things are.

No one can change the way
things are.

Sacred knowledge is like this . . .

Immutable!

Wisdom simply reflects the way
things are.

It goes beyond conventional
knowledge,

Beyond everyday knowledge,

Beyond the knowledge of facts.

Be wary of everyday knowledge,

Be wary of knowledge which claims
objectivity . . .

Unless it is grounded in wisdom.

Can there be true objectivity . . .

In a living world . . .

On a finite planet . . .

Where we are all brothers
and sisters?

Is it not better to go beyond
everyday knowledge,

The knowledge of facts,

And abide by sacred knowledge . . .

The knowledge of the heart . . .

The knowledge of people and life?

Abide by wisdom,
common to all,

Discover within

The sacred power

Of compassion.

To abide by kindness!

To abide by compassion!

This is wisdom . . .

The road to lasting happiness . . .

To bliss.

Kindness, compassion, wisdom,

Power, truth, and love . . .

These are sacred.

These all people share.

Discover them in others . . .

Discover them too in yourself.

Do you wonder, "How shall I discover
the source,

The fountainhead of kindness
and compassion,

Wisdom, power, truth, and love,

Within others and . . .

In myself?"

It is not so hard!

To discover the source of wisdom
and virtue within oneself . . .

Is not really so hard.

For example . . . feel the water
of a shower

On your head,

On your shoulders,

Down your back.

Feel rivulets of water on your body.

Feel the warmth!

Feel the firmness of warm porcelain

Beneath your feet.

This experience . . . this knowledge . . .

Is already sacred somehow.

The awareness of these sensations

Is immediate, forceful,
incontrovertible . . .

It is a kind of knowledge.

Does not everyone experience a
shower . . .

Much the same?

A shower is simply a shower.

This is how it is!

This is the basis of wisdom . . .

Shared knowledge,

Common experiences,

Universality.

Take a shower.

Take a walk in the sunshine . . .

Or in the rain.

Discover wisdom.

Absorb it, and . . .

Abide by it!

Take a walk in the rain or the
sunshine . . .

Feel the water, feel the warmth.

Feel the earth . . .

Feel the wind's breath . . .

Watch the sky!

Note that we can truly experience
these things . . .

Experience them "incontrovertibly" . . .

Only in the present moment,

In the here and now.

That is why, unique, such an experience is sacred.

That is why each moment of eternity . . .

Is likewise holy and sacred.

Everyone in a shower,
in sunshine or in rain,

Feels much the same.

Such wholehearted, such *wholesome*
experiences . . .

Are also sacred,

Partly because they are shared.

Everyone may share experiences
which are similar . . .

"Similar" . . . This means the same but
also different!

The same sensations . . .

Different in context,

Different in time and place.

The wholehearted sharing of
wholesome experiences . . .

From person to person
and in groups,

In communities, in nations,
and cultures . . .

This kind of sharing is sacred.

The wholehearted sharing of
wholesome experiences *directly*,

Through being present together,
here and now,

Through the sharing of context,
of time and place . . .

This is truly sacred.

The wholehearted sharing of
wholesome experiences *indirectly*,

Through communication . . . through
imagination . . .

Through pictures, words, and
sound . . .

This is likewise awesomely sacred.

When you experience something
mindfully . . .

A shower, sunshine, the rain . . .

These are part of truth . . .

Of your truth

And everyone else's.

When we experience things
mindfully . . .

This is holiness.

We are sacred.

That is also partly why

The things we experience
are sacred.

Is it the things which are sacred,

Or the experiences which are sacred?

Pay no attention . . .

This is an irrelevant question.

Things exist . . . We exist!

They are sacred . . . We are sacred!

When sacred meets sacred . . .

Experiences arise . . .

That is all.

If we keep our minds open and allow
them each moment to be filled . . .

Experiences arise that are
wholesome . . .

Experiences arise that are sacred.

Happiness arises and . . .

Wisdom inhabits the mind.

Practice stillness, opening
your mind . . .

Let it be filled anew every moment.

Your happiness depends upon it.

This is what it means to be mindful.

Practice . . . Be mindful!

Sit quietly for a while . . .

Undistracted . . .

Every day.

You exist . . . Other people exist.

All are sacred.

Mindful sharing is joyful . . .

Mindful sharing is especially sacred.

We exist . . . We are sacred!

Every one among us is cherished . . .

Every one is blessed!

All are cherished and blessed by
the sun!

All are blessed and cherished
by the rain!

Think about this . . .

The whole universe has conspired for
countless ages

To bring each one of us into being.

What privilege . . .

What joy!

Take a walk in the rain
or the sunshine.

Experience the time and the place
to the full . . .

Experience everything as it arises
and ceases.

Awaken to each moment . . .

And let it go!

That is how to be happy.

Go beyond each moment . . .
Into the next!

Experience everything to the full
as it happens . . .

And let go.

To experience and let go . . .

This is holiness.

Experience everything to the full
as it happens and let go!

Be happy! Go beyond each
moment . . .

Into the next . . . and the next!

Go beyond the boundaries
of time . . .

Into eternity!

Go beyond each moment!

Go beyond time into eternity . . .

Into bliss!

This is your true home.

Be mindful, wholehearted,
utterly present,

Wholly awake, conscious . . .
wherever you are . . .

And you will be sharing,
communing, with others.

This is holiness.

This is simple holiness,

Of which there will be,

Of which there can be . . .

No end.

Take a moment to pause

And ponder on this.

So, how shall we live . . .

Moment by moment,

Hour by hour,

Day by day?

Explore our options and . . .

Simplify our choices!

Choose what we enjoy and can
do well . . .

Choose to be happy . . .

Choose what will benefit others.

Is this simple enough?

Choose what we do well,

Which benefits others . . .

And we will enjoy their
encouragement . . .

Their praise and their thanks.

We do well to choose
what benefits others,

But not to make their thanks and
their praises our goal . . .

For then we would never be satisfied.

Go beyond the changeable opinions
of others,

Until there is peace in your heart.

Thus, we find our work, our job, our role,

And apply ourselves to it with diligence . . .

Wholeheartedly, with integrity.

We apply ourselves thus, find happiness . . .

And earn our livelihood.

We balance work, endeavor, labor

With recreation . . .

With play and adequate rest.

(And we cultivate friendships.)

If the work is not paid,

Or we have no livelihood,

Our task is to survive . . .

And, if we can, to be happy.

If our work is in the house
or not paid,

We may still do our chores
mindfully! . . . Do them well . . .

Take satisfaction, even pleasure, in
our actions.

We can be thankful at least
for this work and . . .

Discover the virtue of discipline.

If we have no livelihood,
it is easy to feel angry or sad,

But we can still be thankful
for the kindness of others . . .

Discover their generosity . . .

And find gratitude arise in ourselves.

Do you have your health, some food,
clothing, shelter, friendship?

Do you have any occupation . . .

Something . . . anything . . .
worthwhile to do?

Yes . . . Then be thankful!

Be full of thanks!

Be full right to the brim!

Be thankful! Choose happiness!

Give thanks.

Be happy!

Smile!

Smile.

Share your smiles!

Share your joy . . .

And you will be repaying all kindness!

Start an epidemic of smiling.

Share your happiness.

Set the tone for others . . .

See them smile in return.

Share your joy and your smiles
with others.

See them smile and reward you
in turn . . .

With friendship, with food,

With clothing and shelter,

With wherewithal and with work.

If we already have food, clothing,
shelter, friendship,

Wherewithal, and work . . .

We may be happy.

We are blessed . . .

Some would say we are rich!

If we already have food, clothing,
shelter, friendship,

Wherewithal, and work,

Why wait for a smile . . .

Before sharing with others
more needy?

Be quick to be generous,
and this way . . .

Bring a smile to yourself.

Go beyond self-seeking!

Explore your options!

Look for choices that
benefit others.

Help others . . .

But take care to avoid physical . . .

Or emotional exhaustion.

Temper your compassion
with wisdom.

Balance your work, your endeavors,
your labor . . .

Even your charity, your giving . . .

With recreation, with friendship,

With relaxation and play . . .

And with adequate sleep.

We cannot help others if we are exhausted . . .

In body or mind.

Wisdom is kindness . . .

And kindness is wisdom.

Balance the two, if you can.

Wisdom is kindness . . .

And kindness is wisdom.

Our minds already know what this
means . . .

And they know it is true.

What do our minds know?

They know this . . .

As a raindrop is to the ocean,

So human beings are linked . . .

Each one to the remainder.

All beings are linked in many
and various ways.

We are the same but different,

Different but the same . . .

Each is part of the whole!

Have you heard . . .

*"Everyone's blood is red . . .
Everyone's tears are salty"?*

Thus although there are differences,

All people are alike . . .

We are all brothers and sisters!

We are all brothers and sisters.

Therefore the symmetrical logic

Of the mystery that binds us
is this . . .

Harm yourself and you are harming
others . . .

Harm others . . .

And you are undoubtedly harming
yourself!

The logic continues similarly
like this . . .

Help yourself and you are helping
others . . .

Help others,

And you are undoubtedly helping
yourself!

With thoughts, feelings, words,
and actions,

We can help or hinder ourselves . . .

We can help or harm one another.

For happiness' sake, it is as well . . .

To be mindful of this . . .

At all times.

Be mindful! Be aware. Be awake!

Pay attention at all times,
in every moment . . .

To your thoughts . . . feelings . . .

Actions . . . and words!

Be calm, kind, generous, loving!

Watch yourself . . .

As a mother watches over her child!

Ponder this . . .

Our positions, our roles, our
occupations, our jobs . . .

May not form our true life's work.

Our true work may simply be
to look after

First ourselves . . .

Then our brothers and sisters.

Our true work may be to look after ourselves,

And our brothers and sisters

Any way we must . . .

Body, mind, and spirit . . .

Any way we can!

To divide people into "Us" and
"Them," is to make a costly mistake.

There is no "Them," no "Us" . . .

There is no "They" for
or against "We" . . .

For "They" are "Us" . . .

And "We" are "Them"!

All are one . . . together.

Happiness depends on not
taking sides.

On avoiding angry thoughts,
words, and actions.

It is best to be still . . .

To avoid conflict . . .

To go beyond all aggression.

Happiness depends on
doing no harm,

On helping each other without
thought or question . . .

Spontaneously, generously,
indiscriminately . . .

Lovingly.

Happiness depends not only
on helping and doing no harm . . .

But also . . . beforehand, primarily,
foremost . . .

On the intention to help and to do
no harm.

Make these your intentions . . .

And you will win equanimity,

Happiness, peace.

For happiness' sake, keep your
mind clear . . .

Untroubled by feelings of guilt
or shame,

Untroubled by self-seeking!

Give yourself wholly to goodness,

To caring for yourself and for others.

Give yourself to caring for
yourself . . .

In order to care for others.

Be happy!

What is good for you is good for
others . . .

And what is good for others
is good for you.

A warm heart, full of kindness,
compassion . . .

A cool mind, full of the sacred
knowledge of wisdom . . .

Why not cultivate these?

For happiness depends on
a generous heart . . .

And a mind that is still . . .

A mind that is clear . . .

That is all!

For happiness' sake . . . Go beyond.

Go beyond words into calm, stillness,
peace . . .

Go beyond imagination . . .

Go beyond even yourself.

Go beyond life and death . . .

Go beyond time.

Go beyond everything . . . into bliss!

Go beyond everything . . .
Go beyond . . .

Go beyond . . .

Go beyond . . .

Go beyond everything . . .

Into serenity . . .

Bliss!